Carl Memorial Book

Carl: A Mother's Love, A Life Remembered

By

Dr. Johann Richardson, PhD

Dedication

This book is dedicated to my son, Carl David Richardson. Nineteen years was not enough time, but it was enough to leave a mark that violence could not erase. Your life gave my love its deepest meaning. Your loss gave my purpose its voice. Your name carries the work my heart refuses to stop doing. This is for every mother who had to learn how to breathe again.

For every family living in the "after." For every life changed because love chose to endure. Carl, you are gone from my sight, but never from my story.

To all of Carl's friends, who continue to check on us, share their memories, and keep his spirit alive in their hearts, your kindness, love, and remembrance mean more than words can express. You remind us that Carl's light still shines through those who loved him.

Forever my son,

Forever loved.

Acknowledgement

In memory of my son, Carl David Richardson, whose life and love are woven through every page of this book. Your time here was far too short but the impact of your spirit is immeasurable and everlasting.

I acknowledge you not only as my child, but as the heart of this work, the reason I found the strength to write, to remember, and to hope. Your courage, your laughter and your dreams continue to guide me, even in your absence.

This book stands as a testament to your life, a way to say that you were here, you mattered, and you are loved beyond words. Every acknowledgement, every line, and every lesson within these pages is offered in your honor.

Table of Contents

Prologue

The Day the World Changed

On March 27, 2014, time did not stop; I did. The world around me kept moving, cars passed by, people continued breathing, living, laughing, and existing. But my heart, my heart was ripped wide open and left bleeding in a place no one could see.

That was the day my son, my beautiful Carl, was taken from this world. And though this story ends here, in a silence that still haunts my bones, it truly begins long before this day of unimaginable loss.

To understand the depth of my grief, you must first understand the immensity of my love. And to understand my love, we must return to the beginning, to the moment Carl's existence became the quiet miracle I had begged the heavens for.

The Power of A Mother's Love

A mother's love for her son is unlike any other, and when my nineteen-year-old son's life was stolen, that love became the truth I live with, tender, fierce, and forever unbroken.

Chapter 1

Before the Beginning

The first spark of life, hope, and unwavering belief

Carl, your dad and I longed for you long before we even knew it could happen. That November, around Thanksgiving, we decided we were ready to bring a new heartbeat into our lives. Weeks later, in early December, the first wave of nausea confirmed what my heart already knew: I was carrying you. I remember the mixture of fear and elation, the quiet trembling as I whispered the news to your father. His face lit up for a moment, and then fell as the doctor's first words sank in: "You're not pregnant."

I remember the flicker of disappointment in his eyes, the way he looked at me with both hope and heartbreak. Even the doctor's pity made my chest ache. But inside me, I was certain. There was life within me, and I clung to that certainty like a lifeline. A few days later, the blood test confirmed it. You were growing inside me, tiny and perfect, and the love I already felt for you was infinite.

From that moment, I began speaking to you, whispering hopes and dreams even before you had words. I imagined your laughter, your curiosity, your little hands, and I already felt you shaping our family. Every breath I took, every flutter of anticipation in my body, carried the promise of you.

And from that moment on, I believed in you with every beat of my heart.

Chapter 2

The First Flutter of Forever

Tiny kicks and first connections that whispered love

The first time I felt your tiny kicks, it was barely more than a whisper beneath my heart. The flutter startled me into awe, like the smallest secret being spoken from inside my body. Each subtle movement, each gentle nudge reminded me that you were alive and thriving, already communicating with me in a language only a mother and child can understand.

As the weeks passed, your movements grew stronger and surer, almost as if you were learning to dance to the rhythm of my heartbeat. Sometimes your kicks arrived like surprises, sharp enough to steal my breath for a moment, yet each one was a blessing, proof that you were there, living, growing, reaching for me in your own way. In those quiet shared moments, I felt the first magic of motherhood take root, a knowing, wordless connection that existed long before I ever saw your face.

Pregnancy was not gentle to me. For nine long months, nausea clung to me without mercy. I woke sick, lived sick, and slept sick, and yet I carried each wave of discomfort with a strange kind of gratitude. Your big sister watched me with worried eyes far older than her years, always ready to fetch the candies that helped ease the sickness for just a moment. Her tiny hands and her small acts of care became a quiet love story between you two long before you ever met.

Each evening, when your father came home from work, he placed his hands over the place where you lived, his voice softening as he spoke to you. He believed, as we all did, that you were a girl. We even called you "Carla," lovingly and confidently, as if naming you helped us hold you closer. Your siblings joined in, arguing playfully, each certain they knew your secret. But during every sonogram, you kept your legs tucked tightly, guarding your truth until the very end. Your brother, in the end, was the one who guessed right.

For forty weeks, I carried not just your small forming body but the dream of who you would become. Every flutter and every twist beneath my ribs felt like a promise, a heartbeat of tomorrow. You were more than life growing inside me. You were hope, anticipation, and wonder. You were ours before we ever saw you, loved before we ever held you, known before we ever spoke your name.

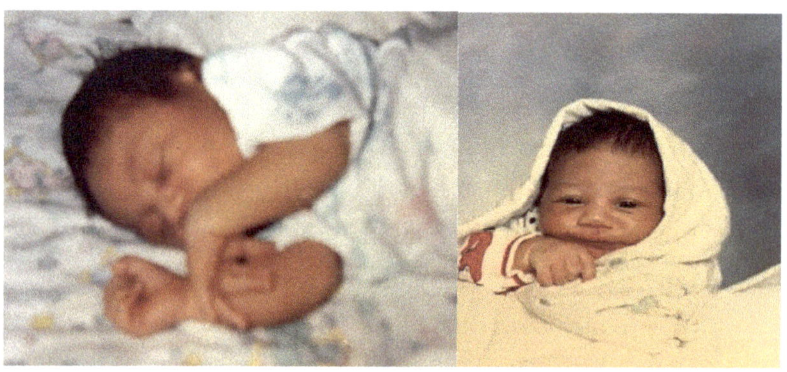

Chapter 3

The Day the Earth Stood Still

The day the world paused for your first breath.

When your birthday finally came, August 19, 1994, the world seemed to pause. The moment I saw you, time folded in on itself. My heart knew you before my eyes did. The joy that flooded me was so deep; it felt like the earth itself was singing your name.

Your dad saw you first. He helped bring you into this world, hands trembling with awe as he cut your umbilical cord. In his joy, he ran from nurse to doctor, giving grateful hugs and kisses, as if no gratitude could ever be enough for the miracle we had just witnessed.

You, our shining star, had finally arrived. So perfect, so luminous. An angel wrapped in soft blankets and new beginnings. Your dad gave you his first name, Carl, and your grandfather's as your middle name. That is how you became our beloved Carl David Richardson, the heart of our family, the soul we had been waiting for all along.

In your first cries, your first breaths, I felt a love so profound it became the axis of our universe. The world was brighter, fuller, and infinitely more beautiful simply because you had arrived.

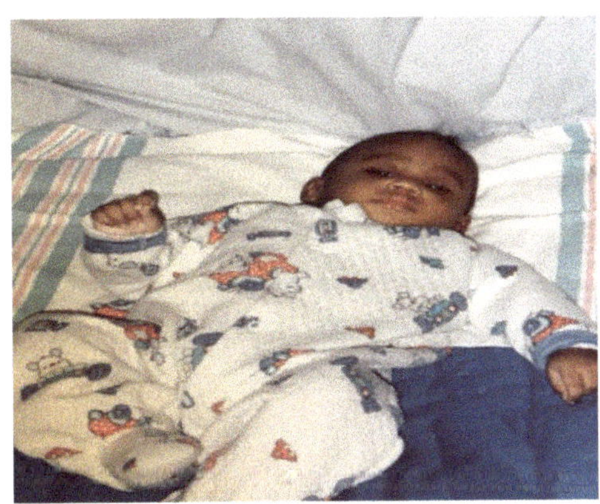

Chapter 4

A Love That Learned to Breathe

The tender rhythm of early life and the quiet shaping of our bond

The bond between us grew immeasurably when you began breastfeeding. Each moment you nursed felt like a quiet conversation between our souls, a rhythm only we could understand. Yet, as you neared three months, something within you began to change. You would turn away from my breast with a look of pure distaste, as if the milk that once comforted you had suddenly lost its magic.

Your father tried to help, gently encouraging you to nurse, but your tiny face said everything. The grimace you made, so dramatic, as though tasting something unbearably sour, had us both laughing through our surprise. Still, beneath that laughter was an ache. My heart knew our time in that tender ritual was ending, even before my mind accepted it. So, with a bit of sadness and love interwoven, I began giving you formula, sensing this was your way of telling me you were ready for something new.

Carl, as you grew, I began to see how truly extraordinary you were. Even as a baby, there was something peaceful and knowing in your eyes. You rarely cried. Instead, you greeted the world with quiet smiles that seemed to come from a place of gentle understanding. Many mornings I would wake before dawn, thinking you were still asleep, only to peek into your crib and find you already awake, gazing around as if you were taking in life itself. When I softly said, "Good morning, baby," you would look up at me and smile, as though you understood every word. You filled our home with pure joy from the very beginning.

Your brother and sister adored you in ways that only children, full of wonder, can. They would race home from school each day, eager to hold you, to feed you, to help in any way they could. To them, you weren't just their baby brother, you were a little miracle they wanted to protect and surround with love. I often smiled watching them hover close whenever I bathed you or changed your clothes, afraid to let you out of their sight. Before you came along, they couldn't wait to run outside and play. But after you arrived, their world shifted. Nothing mattered more to them than being near you. You brought us all together in a new and beautiful way; your quiet presence reminded us what love truly feels like.

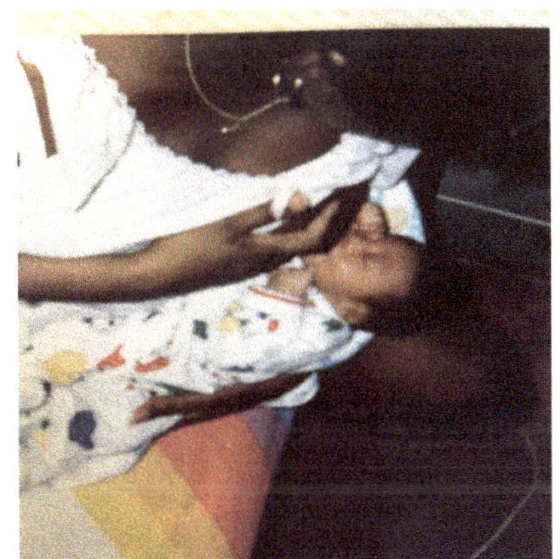
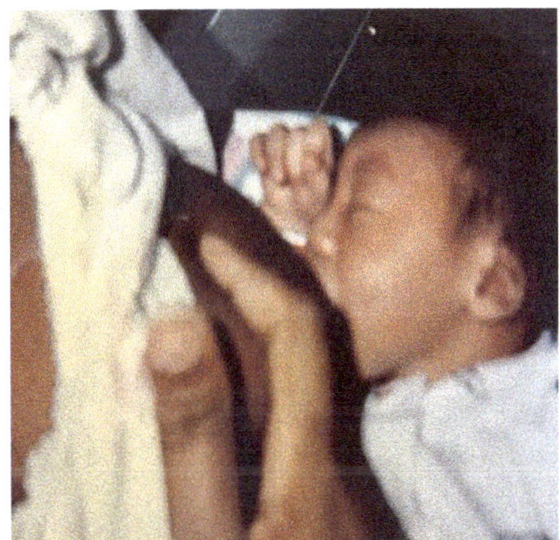

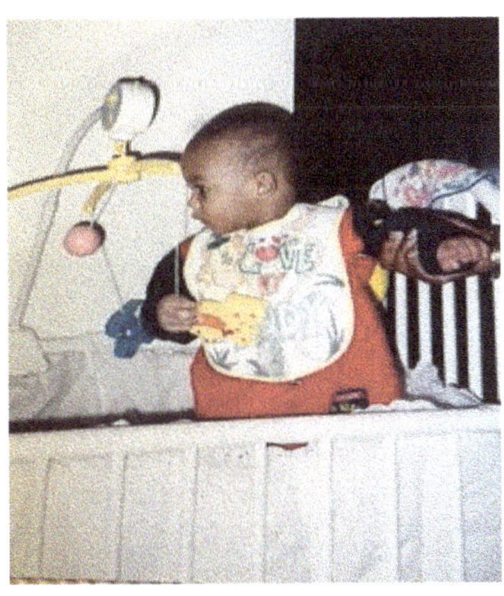

Carl: A Mother's Love, A Life Remembered

Carl with his brother, sister and on a train with uncle pops

Chapter 5

A Home Filled with Laughter

Joy that filled the walls, music in the pots and pans, and hearts intertwined

Carl, you always had a mischievous sparkle in your eyes. One of my favorite memories is the day we found you sitting in the middle of the room, covered head to toe in Vaseline after emptying an entire jar onto your hair and face. We couldn't stop laughing. Your slippery little grin made it impossible to be upset. It took ages to get that Vaseline out, and in the end, I had to cut your hair. Even so, that day remains one of those moments that still make me smile, a memory filled with laughter, love, and your little spark that made our home so full of life.

There's one memory that always stands out, even after all these years, and it still makes me smile. Your dad had this little wart on his thumb, and for some reason, you loved to squeeze it. If he said "ouch," you would burst into the most infectious laughter, laughing until your eyes watered. You were the same way whenever one of us tripped, laughing as if it were the funniest thing in the world. I could never understand what you found so amusing, but your laughter filled the house and made it impossible not to laugh along.

There was another thing, too. If your dad had even the smallest hole in one of his T-shirts, you would find it right away. You'd poke your finger through and wiggle it until the hole grew bigger. You never did that to anyone else, just your dad. Something about the two of you had a quiet, unspoken bond that showed even in those small, silly moments.

I'll never forget when your grandfather came from Jamaica to visit us for the first time and met you. It was love at first sight. You connected instantly, as if you had known each other forever. He spent almost all six weeks of his visit with you, and though your brother and sister got less of his time, they didn't seem to mind. You all adored him, and your laughter filled those weeks with joy.

When it came time for your grandfather to return to Jamaica, I knew it would be hard for you. I tried to prepare you, and so did he, but nothing could make it easy. After he left, I found you in the room where he had stayed, lying on his bed, crying quietly. My heart ached watching you grieve that goodbye, and I sat beside you, crying too. That moment has stayed with me all these years, a tender reminder of how deeply you love and how much your heart can hold.

Over the years, your grandfather continued to visit, and with each visit, you came to understand the rhythm of it, the joy of his arrival, the gentle ache of his departure, and the comforting promise that he would always return.

I remember taking you to Jamaica for the first time. You fell in love with the island, the warmth of the air, the laughter that followed us everywhere, and the way the family seemed to greet you with open arms no matter where we went. My family lives across different parts of Jamaica, so we traveled from city to city, sharing stories, meals, and the easy joy that only home can bring. Everyone who met you adored you, and your smile seemed to belong to the island itself.

We made that journey many times after, you and I, always eager to reunite with the people and places that held so much love for us. Those trips became a part of us, a thread woven through our memories, sweet and lasting, like the song of the sea along the Jamaican coast.

Dr. Johann Richardson, PhD

Carl and his dad

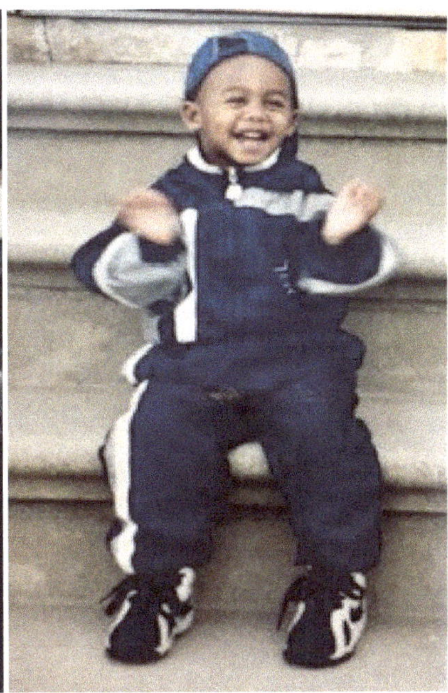

Carl & family

Carl's Jamaican Grandfather

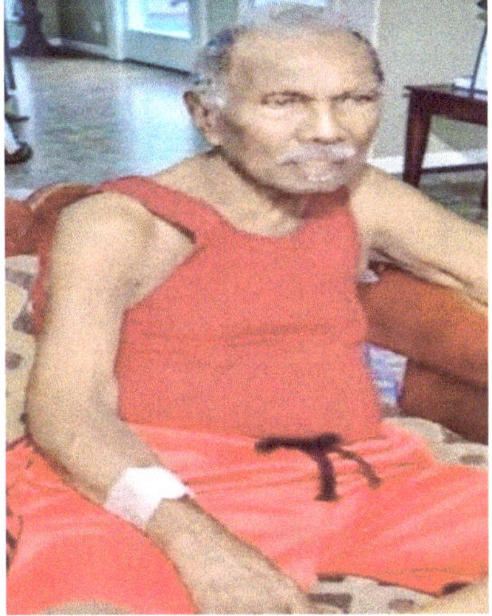

Chapter 6

Little Goodbyes, Big Hellos

First separations, tender attachments, and the gentle rhythm of daily life

Daycare was a new world, and you met it in your own tender way. Some mornings, leaving you felt like breaking a piece of my own heart. I can still see your face pressed against the glass door as I walked away, your small hand lifted, your eyes wide with longing.

But every afternoon, when I returned, your joy was a light that erased the ache of morning. You would run into my arms, your whole body warm with excitement, as if time had paused just for this reunion.

On our walk home, you always found ways to make me laugh. You would beg to be carried, and when I told you, "No, baby, you are a big boy now," you would suddenly stop, lift one leg, and tell me with a serious little face, "Mommy, my foot is broken, I cannot walk." I can still hear that mischievous tone and see that twinkle in your eyes. I would laugh so hard tears would stream down my cheeks, your clever little trick melting my heart every time.

Later, when your dad came home, I would retell the story, and we would laugh together, marveling at your playful spirit, your clever mind, and your boundless charm. Those days were full of love, laughter, and the kind of moments that stay in a mother's heart forever.

Your daycare teacher, Ms. Marva, became another steady presence in your early life. Her kindness, her patience, and the way she saw your gentleness were gifts she gave both of us.

Carl, you always had such a gentle heart. Every evening after daycare, no matter how much of a hurry I was in to get home and start dinner, you insisted on stopping to see our dear neighbor, Ms. Palomino. It became your little ritual, your moment of joy before the evening settled in. She would greet you with that warm smile, already ready with your favorite treat, a small handful of grapes. You loved them so much, and she loved you enough to always have them waiting.

I will never forget the day we stopped by and she did not have any grapes. She looked at you, a bit flustered, and said softly, "Baby, I have no grapes today. Would you like an apple instead?" Your little face fell, and with that earnest honesty only a child can have, you said, "You know I am coming and you did not buy grapes?" For a moment, I wanted to scold you, but before I could, Ms. Palomino laughed that kind, knowing laugh. She said, "I am sorry, baby. Tomorrow I will have grapes for you." And she did.

She adored you, Carl. In her eyes, you were like a grandson. In your heart, she was more than just a neighbor. She was a piece of family built through kindness and routine. Even as a small child, you moved people with your sweetness, your sincerity, your love. You had a way of leaving gentle marks on the hearts around you, without even realizing it.

You were loved everywhere you went. Even then, you carried a light that people wanted to hold.

Carl's teacher, Ms. Marva, at Daycare

Carl: A Mother's Love, A Life Remembered

Carl and his mother

Chapter 7

Adventures, Family, and First Birthdays

Family trips, milestones, and the blossoming of a child are cherished

Our little family loved to wander, and every road trip to North & South Carolina became its own adventure, suitcases packed tight, snacks tucked into bags, and your siblings buzzing with excitement. You, Carl, were always the calmest among us, wide-eyed and curious, taking everything in as if the world were a storybook waiting to be read.

When we reached the warm embrace of family, you were home. Your grandparents held you as if you were made of light. Aunts and uncles circled you with affection, your cousins tugged you along in their games, and love poured over you like sunshine. Your first birthday was more than a milestone; it was a celebration of the joy you brought into every room. You sat in your high chair, eyes sparkling as everyone sang to you. When the cake arrived, your hands dove right in, smearing sweetness across your cheeks. The laughter that followed felt like heaven cracking open just to bless us. You were surrounded by love, layer after layer of it, and I held onto that moment as tightly as I held onto you.

As the months turned into years, those early memories became the roots of your story, steady, warm, and full of wonder. I remember the way you reached for the world: the first time you stumbled across the grass barefoot, the way you chased bubbles through the yard, how your giggles filled the air like music. You had a way of reminding us to slow down, to see beauty in the small things, a dandelion, a sunset, a raindrop sliding down the window.

Every family trip became another page in our book. Long car rides turned into sing-along; detours became hidden adventures. You watched your siblings from your car seat, delighting in their noise and energy, while I caught glimpses of your reflection smiling back at me in the rearview mirror, a quiet joy that made the miles seem shorter. Your first birthday was just the beginning of many celebrations, each one whispering the same truth: our lives were brighter because of you. Growth came quickly, as it often does, but through every change, every scraped knee, every bedtime story, every shared laugh, the same love surrounded you, unchanging and strong. Family, adventure, and the wonder of your earliest years became the foundation of everything that followed.

Carl and his Grandparents in North Carolina

Dr. Johann Richardson, PhD

The Doctor who delivered you

Chapter 8

The Tender Work of Letting Go

Coming of age through a mother's eyes

Carl, watching you grow into yourself was like witnessing a sunrise, slow, steady, and impossibly beautiful. There were moments when I would look at you and see traces of the sweet little boy who smeared cake across his cheeks, who called for your daddy in the middle of the night, who filled our home with playful mischief and laughter. But more and more, I saw the man you were becoming, a young man with a gentle strength, a thoughtful mind, and a heart that felt deeply.

When you started first grade at PS 181, we were filled with excitement and a touch of nervousness. Mrs. Specktor was your teacher that year. You told us some children did not like her because she could be strict, but you did. You said she took the time to explain things carefully, and you loved that about her. When she suggested you join the afterschool program, she thought you needed more help. Once you began, your teacher there quickly realized something different. She told us you already understood the lessons and could see how bright and curious you were. That afterschool teacher happened to be Ms. Joyner. Instead of sending you home, she saw potential in you and decided to keep you on so you could help her teach the other children. That was the beginning of something special.

When second grade began, we were both surprised and delighted to learn that Ms. Joyner would be your teacher again. You already shared a connection, so walking into her classroom felt like coming home. Every afternoon, you would rush through the door, eager to tell me everything that happened that day, what you learned, who you sat next to, and what Ms. Joyner said. I will never forget when she told me,

"Carl is the kind of child I know will do well. He is so attentive to his work." You took that to heart. Every day after school, you would sit at the table and finish your homework before anything else. You wanted to make her proud.

Fifth grade brought Ms. Bertard, another teacher who left a lasting mark on you. She was firm but deeply caring, the kind of teacher who saw who you could become and refused to let you settle for less. She made sure you stayed on top of every assignment, and I trusted her completely. I remember telling her that when you were in school, she was responsible for you, and she embraced that fully. She took you under her wing, guiding you as if you were her own child.

Those school days were full, but they were beautiful. I signed you up for all sorts of activities, Little League baseball with the Rosedale team, tennis, and basketball at Roy Wilkins Park on Saturday mornings. I loved watching you play under the bright sun, your face glowing with joy and determination. They offered swimming too, but you decided against it because you said it did not feel right taking lessons when other children needed them more and because you already had a pool at home. That was you, always thoughtful, even then.

Every Wednesday afternoon, we would drive to Bayside for piano lessons. At first, you were not excited about them. You told me you were doing it for me. But as the weeks passed, your reluctance softened, replaced by quiet pride each time your fingers found the melody. Over time, you began to look forward to those lessons. Watching that change filled me with quiet joy.

From the moment you left for junior high at St. Clare's, my heart quietly marked each milestone you reached. Every morning, I cherished our time together as I took you to school, and no matter the day's challenges, I made sure to be there to pick you up when classes ended, a rhythm that became our gentle tradition, one I kept through every school you attended. These years gifted you with lifelong friends and lessons woven deep into the fabric of your heart. I took comfort in seeing you grow in faith, especially as we shared each Sunday in church together, surrounded by the warmth of community and the belief that had shaped me as a child.

St. Clare's was more than just your school. It was the place where you learned about Christ in ways I had always hoped for you. Sometimes, you came home with bright eyes, excited to share stories from Mass and new Bible verses, showing me that faith was becoming your own. My greatest wish was to instill in you the love and teachings I had received about Christianity, so we chose a path for you that reflected the importance this faith holds in our lives.

Looking back, the days at St. Clare's set the pace for who you would become. The friendships you made are still an anchor in your life, each one a testament to those sweet formative years. Graduation arrived in a blur of joy and pride, but not before you attended your first prom. Your dad and I watched you walk out the door, radiant and growing, bringing Kai, your first prom date, into that special night. Through every memory, through every gentle act, my love wrapped around you, quiet and unwavering, just as a mother's love always does.

There are moments in life when the gentle warmth of a mother's love wraps around you so completely that even years later, the memory feels like a soft embrace from home itself.

The moment high school came around, we chose St. John's Preparatory School. It was not our first choice. The school we wanted most had no openings for you, but we believed in keeping you close, even though it meant adjusting our expectations and plans.

High school changed you in quiet ways. Not loud, not sudden, just small shifts that only a mother would notice. Your voice deepened, your shoulders broadened, and your confidence stepped forward, as though it had always been waiting inside you. But what touched me most was not the physical changes; it was the goodness that grew stronger in you every year.

You became the kind of friend people trusted, the one they called when their world felt heavy. You were the boy who never turned away from someone in need, even when no one else was watching. I remember the way your teachers spoke of you with respect in their voices, not just for your mind, but for your character.

You had this quiet determination that made me proud every single day. You were focused, your goals clear, your dreams reaching beyond what you ever said out loud. But I saw it all, Carl. A mother always sees.

What I did not see, what I never could have prepared for, was how quickly time would slip through my fingers. One day, you were asking me to read your bedtime stories, and the next, you were standing before your senior year, tall and radiant, wearing the confidence of a young man who knew exactly who he was.

I would watch you leaving the house in the morning, your backpack slung over one shoulder, your headphones in, walking with that easy rhythm that was all yours. Some mornings, I opened my mouth to call after you, not for anything important, just to hold onto one more moment. But I did not. I let you grow. I let you walk into the world the way you wanted to, even though my heart still saw you as the little boy who wanted grapes from Ms. Palomino every evening.

That is the tenderness of a mother's love. Letting go even when my arms ache to hold on.

And Carl, every step you took into that world made me proud. Proud of the man you were becoming, proud of how you carried yourself, proud of how you treated others. You were growing, stretching, stepping into the fullness of your purpose, even before you knew how short your time would be.

Your laughter, your kindness, your gentle courage, they were all blooming inside you. And I, your mother, felt that quiet, aching joy of watching you grow, never imagining that these memories would one day become the threads I would cling to in the dark.

Because love has a way of saving us long before we know we will need saving.

And you, Carl, were saving me every day without even trying.

You had a gift for connecting with others, especially children in the neighborhood. You gladly spend your afternoons tutoring them, patient, encouraging, and full of warmth, turning every lesson into a moment of confidence and growth. Whether it was helping with math homework or reading stories, you made learning feel possible and fun. Your calm spirit and kindness left a mark on every child you helped, a quiet legacy of care, compassion, and community.

Carl Tutoring

Dr. Johann Richardson, PhD

PS 181 Principal Ms. Auguste

St. Clair's Prom

Carl: A Mother's Love, A Life Remembered

St. John's Prep Brest Cancer walk & Graduation

Chapter 9

Watching You Cross the Threshold

Dreams, Purpose and widening worlds

There comes a moment in every mother's life when she realizes her child is no longer a child.

Not because of a birthday, or a milestone, or a cap and gown, but because of a look, a moment, a shift so gentle you only understand it later.

For me, that moment came with you, Carl, during your last years of high school.

You were standing in the kitchen, pouring juice into a glass, sunlight touching your face just right. You weren't talking, you weren't laughing; you weren't doing anything extraordinary, yet something in you had changed. You were taller, yes, but it was more than height. There was a calmness about you, a quiet certainty, a steadiness. A maturity I didn't see coming until it was already there.

I looked at you and thought,

My son is becoming a man.

And with that realization came pride, joy, and a small, tender grief, the grief every mother feels as she watches her baby grow wings.

In those years, your world began widening in ways you embraced with open arms. You worked hard in school, but you worked just as hard at becoming yourself. You made decisions with a sense of responsibility that always impressed me. You were careful, thoughtful, and intentional. Even your friends saw it, how you held yourself, how you carried the weight of your future with a grace far beyond your age.

Carl: A Mother's Love, A Life Remembered

You had dreams, Carl. Quiet ones, but powerful.
Sometimes, on our drives home from school, you would open up in ways that made my heart swell. You would talk about your plans, college, a career, and the life you imagined building. You didn't brag; you didn't rush; you simply knew who you were meant to be.

I could feel your "why" taking shape, even then.

And yet, even as adulthood approached, you held onto pieces of childhood that kept your spirit soft. The way you would sit with your siblings, laughing until your eyes watered. The way you still hugged me tight after school, almost lifting me off the ground. The way you called out "Mom!" from across the house with that familiar melody in your voice, half boy, half man, all heart.

Those were the moments that reminded me that no matter how tall you grew, you would always, in some secret place, be my little boy.

As you reached eighteen and then nineteen, I began to watch you differently. Not out of worry, though a mother always worries, but out of awe. You had stepped into your own manhood with dignity, humility, and compassion. You navigated life with a kindness that felt rare in this world.

There were days I would stand at the window, watching you walk down the driveway, and a sudden wave of tenderness would wash over me. I would pray silently:
God, keep him. Protect him. Let him see every dream he chases. Let him live the life he is meant to live.

I didn't know then what I know now, that prayers sometimes become the very thing a mother clings to when the world shatters.

But in those days, I loved you in the present moment.
I loved you with a sweetness that felt simple and safe.

I loved you without fear of losing you, because how could I imagine a world where your laughter was no longer echoing through our home?

You were on the threshold of adulthood, standing at the doorway of your future, and I was standing behind you with the soft, unshakeable love of a mother, proud, grateful, and blissfully unaware that time, so generous then, was running faster than my heart could beat.

Carl with his brother, sister and mom

Chapter 10

The Day My Nightmare Became Real

That was the day my heart forgot how to beat without him.

I was just a few blocks from home when the phone rang. One ring, then two. By the third, my pulse had already quickened, and the sound was louder than the hum of the engine. The name on the dashboard screen, Franklin General Hospital, seemed to glow brighter than everything else around it. For a split second, I hesitated. Then I pressed the button on the steering wheel with a damp finger.

"Hello?" My voice sounded normal, but nothing inside me felt normal.

The silence that followed was wrong, too thick, and too heavy. I could hear faint beeps, distant voices, and papers shifting. A hum, like someone was deciding how to break something fragile.

"Is this Mrs. Richardson?"

"Yes."

"This is the emergency department at Franklin General Hospital. Your son Carl has been brought in. He's in trauma. You need to come right away."

The words didn't land all at once. They floated around me, disconnected, like scraps of a conversation I wasn't meant to hear. By the time they sank in, my throat had gone dry. My foot eased off the gas, and the car started to drift. The world outside, the passing houses, the sunlight flickering across the glass, blurred into streaks of color.

I think I said "Okay." Or maybe I didn't say anything at all. I remember the metallic taste of fear in my mouth and the way my hands shook so badly the wheel slid beneath them. I could hear my own heartbeat, hard and uneven, as if my body already knew what my mind refused to believe.

When I reached home, I barely remember getting out of the car. I called for my husband, my cousin-in-law, and my oldest grandson. No one asked for details; they could see everything written on my face. We drove to the hospital in silence, the kind of silence that feels alive, breathing between people who are too afraid to speak the truth out loud.

At the emergency room, they didn't tell us to wait. They guided us to a small room off to the side, quiet and closed. The nurse's voice was soft, her eyes careful. My heart thudded in my chest, each beat hard enough to hurt.

Then the doctors came in. Too many of them, moving in a slow line, their faces drawn, their eyes dark with sympathy. One asked us to sit. I sat. My husband didn't.

The doctor started to speak. His mouth moved, but the words reached me late, like a delay in a bad connection. And then he said to us, those four words that tore the world in two.

"He didn't make it."

For a long moment, everything stopped. The walls, the voices, the air itself, gone. Then a sound escaped me, a sound that didn't even feel human, like something being ripped from the inside out. My knees gave way. The next thing I knew, I was on the floor, surrounded by white shoes and soft voices. Later, they told me my husband had collapsed too, that our grief struck at the same instant, as if our hearts had broken in unison.

The drive home was a blur. I stared out the window, watching the streetlights twist into long, bleeding lines of gold. I kept whispering to myself, this isn't real. This can't be real. At every turn, I half expected to wake up, to find Carl in his room, his voice floating through the hallway.

But reality has a cruel kind of permanence. When I stepped through my front door, the same walls, the same furniture, the same familiar smells were there, but they belonged to a different world now, one where my son no longer existed.

The First Hour at Home

When we returned home, the air inside felt different, heavy, almost alive with absence. The walls seemed closer, pressing in. I walked through each room like a stranger in my own house, my eyes scanning for something, anything, that would prove this was all a terrible mistake. His shoes are by the door. His jacket was slung over the back of a chair. His favorite mug is still sitting on the counter; a faint ring of coffee dried at the bottom.

I touched everything. I needed to. The fabric of his jacket still held his scent, clean detergent and something faintly sweet, like the soap he always used. I pressed it to my face and inhaled until my chest ached, as if breathing him in could somehow bring him back.

People say grief comes in waves, but that first night it didn't come in waves; it came all at once. It hit me like a storm I couldn't see or prepare for. One minute I was standing in the kitchen, staring at the untouched mug, and the next, my knees gave way. I ended up on the cold tile floor, my palms flat against it, and the sound of my own crying echoed through the quiet.

My husband tried to hold me, but I couldn't be still. I remember breaking free from his arms, pacing through the house like a woman possessed, calling Carl's name over and over. I opened his bedroom door, half-expecting to find him there. The room was dim, untouched, frozen in time. Clothes were piled on his chair. A video game was still blinking on his console. There was a faint smell of his cologne in the air.

I sat on his bed and let the memories come: his first steps, his shy smile when he lost his first tooth, the sound of his laughter chasing down the hallway. Each memory cut deeper than the last. The ache in my chest wasn't metaphorical; it was physical, sharp and crushing, as if my heart were splintering piece by piece.

At some point in the night, I found myself in his closet, holding one of his hoodies, rocking back and forth. I whispered to God, to the universe, to Carl, please, please, just let this be a dream. But the world stayed silent.

Outside, morning crept in quietly, uncaring. The sunrise spilled through the blinds, painting soft gold across his empty bed. It was cruel, that light, how it touched everything but him.

By the time I looked up, hours had passed. My body felt hollow, my tears spent, my voice raw. I had never known that pain could live in every part of you, your chest, your bones, your breath. The house was still, yet I could feel him everywhere, like his spirit lingered in the air, watching, waiting, unwilling to leave me entirely alone.

That was the moment reality settled in, not like a blow, but like the slow tightening of a thread around my heart. He was gone. My son was gone. The world would continue to spin, people would laugh, days would pass, but some parts of me had stopped moving forever.

That night, alone in the dark, I pressed my face into my hands and begged God to bring him back, to rewind time, to take me instead. But the only answer was silence. The kind of silence that fills your chest until you can hardly breathe.

That was the night I truly understood what it means to have your heart broken beyond repair.

The days that followed dissolved into a blur of tears and soft voices, food I couldn't eat, sleep that wouldn't come. People came and went, bringing love I couldn't feel. The house was filled with condolences, but not with the one thing I wanted most, his laughter, his warmth, his life.

The family with Councilman Donavan Richards a speech of forgiveness.

Johann's Reflection on Carl and Shenique

I still remember the first time Carl told me about Shenique. His voice carried a quiet joy, the kind that mothers recognize instantly. He said she made him feel "settled," that being with her felt natural, like breathing. When I finally met her, I understood exactly what he meant.

She arrived that evening with a bouquet of fresh flowers and a smile that could soften even the hardest day. There was something graceful about her, but also real, she laughed easily, listened deeply, and treated everyone as though she'd known them forever. I saw right away how much Carl adored her. You could hear it in his tone, see it in his eyes. He was a man of gentle strength, and in Shenique, he had found peace.

Carl Sr. and I took to her almost immediately. She asked my husband about his job, as Carl had told her his dad works as a train conductor for MTA and soon the two of them were discussing everything about train rides as if they had known each other for years. Over time, she became more than Carl's girlfriend, she became family. She'd call me just to talk, sometimes asking about recipes or sharing stories about her day. I looked forward to those moments more than I can say.

When Carl passed on March 27, 2014, everything changed. No parent can ever be prepared for that kind of loss. The grief was heavy, endless, but in the midst of it, my heart broke again when I saw Shenique's pain. She had loved him so completely. Her laughter, once so light, carried a quiet sorrow after that day. She stood beside us through the tears and memories, holding on to every story, every photograph, every small reminder of the man who had meant the world to her.

Even now, I think of how deeply Carl loved her, and how fiercely she loved him back. That kind of bond doesn't fade with time or tragedy, it endures. In every way that mattered, Shenique was and will always be part of our family, a beautiful piece of Carl's story that lives on in our hearts.

Carl: A Mother's Love, A Life Remembered

Carl and his girlfriend Shenique

Chapter 11

The Year of Firsts Without You

Love learning to carry grief in the 'after

Some years divide a life in half:

Before and *after*.

This was the first year that belonged entirely to the *after*.

It began quietly, without ceremony, slipping into January with cold air that felt heavier than winters before it. Even the sky seemed reluctant, muted, the color of old cotton. I moved through the days like a woman learning to walk again, slow, unsteady, unsure if the ground wanted to hold me.

Because every "first" without you was waiting like a shadow around a corner.

The first birthday you didn't have.

The first holiday where your name hovered unspoken in the room.

The first time someone asked me, "How many children do you have?" and I had to choose between honesty and survival.

Grief is not a season you pass through; it is a climate you learn to breathe in.

But the year unfolded regardless, stubborn in its insistence that time must move even when you don't.

The First Spring without You

When spring finally arrived, the world dared to bloom.

Dogwoods opened like soft paper lanterns. Grass returned in deeper greens than I remembered. The air tasted new, almost sweet. And I found myself angry at it for daring to be beautiful.

I stood outside one morning, the sun warm on my shoulders, and whispered into the breeze,

"How can the world grow when my son no longer does?"

No one answered.

But a single leaf drifted down from nowhere, spinning slow circles toward my feet.

I picked it up. Turned it in my hand. And realized that even in beauty, there is falling.

I didn't know then that grief and spring have something in common:

both insist on transformation, whether you're ready or not.

The First Time I Laughed Again

It happened by accident, an unexpected burst, small but startling. Someone told a joke, something simple, and nothing special. And before I could stop myself, a sound escaped me, something like a laugh, though it felt foreign, like a language I had forgotten.

The room went quiet.

Someone looked at me as if I had broken the rules of mourning.

But grief is not a prison cell. It's a landscape. And sometimes, unexpectedly, a wildflower grows between the rocks.

Later that night, guilt washed over me.

How dare I laugh when you could not?

How dare joy rise in a place so broken?

But then a softer voice whispered inside me,

Maybe healing doesn't betray him. Maybe it honors him.

I didn't believe it yet, but I wanted to.

The First Time I Spoke Your Name without Crying

This was the hardest, strangest milestone.

Your name had become a fragile thing; if I touched it, it shattered into tears.

But one evening, while talking to someone who had never met you, I said it:

your name, clear and steady, like offering a piece of myself.

"*My son,*" I began, and for the first time, my voice didn't break.

It felt like standing on legs that had finally remembered how to hold me.

Later, the tears came, but not the drowning kind. These were quieter, warmer tears that came not from pain, but from love remembering its own strength.

The First Dream Where You Were Alive Again

It happened in late summer.

You were standing in the kitchen, the one you used to raid at midnight, wearing that hoodie with the frayed cuffs. You were smiling, leaning against the counter, your arms crossed like you used to do when pretending to be annoyed.

I touched your cheek in the dream. It was warm.

You laughed that soft, breathy laugh.

And for a moment, one breathtaking moment, I believed you were still here.

When I woke up, grief hit me like a wave pulled back too far then slammed into shore.

But beneath the ache was something new, something I hadn't felt since before the world broke open.

Relief.

Because the dream had reminded me: my love hadn't lost you completely. Not really.

Memory has its own resurrection.

The First Winter That Didn't Destroy Me

By the time the next winter arrived, I realized something had shifted.

Not healed, healing is a word too tidy for a wound like this.

But something had rearranged inside me.

The cold still hurt, but it no longer swallowed me whole.

The nights were still long, but they weren't endless.

This time, I decorated the house.

Not because I felt festive, but because I needed light, any light, to push back the dark.

And as I hung one small ornament on a branch, I whispered,

"This is for you.

This light.

This moment.

This love that refuses to die."

The tree shimmered back at me, gentle, golden, steady.

And in the quiet glow, I realized what the year had been trying to teach me:

Grief does not lessen love.

Love carries grief.

And somehow, impossibly, miraculously, love survives.

Carl with his brother and sister

Chapter 12

The Weight of Your Things

Objects hold memory, but love holds the soul

There comes a time after a loss when objects begin to betray you.

At first, they feel sacred, untouchable relics of a life interrupted. You guard them fiercely, as if they were pieces of his body, his breath, his laughter. A shirt still carrying the faintest echo of his scent. A pair of shoes with laces still knotted from the last day he wore them. Notes he scribbled in the margins of a notebook, letters looping and slanted, proof that his hands once moved in this world.

But something happens as time moves, slow and merciless:

his things begin to grow heavy.

Not physically, emotionally, or spiritually.

As if each object asks a question, you cannot yet answer.

What will become of me now?

How long will I hold on?

When will I let me go?

The Closet I Couldn't Open

For months, his closet stayed closed.

It became a sealed room inside a room, a sanctuary where the air hadn't learned he was gone. I'd walk past it, sometimes touching the handle lightly, my fingers resting there as if they could absorb some remnant of warmth from the other side.

But I never opened it.

Grief has a way of turning an ordinary door into a battlefield.

One day, without planning to, I opened it.

Not bravely. Not ceremonially.

Just because my hand, tired of trembling, turned the knob.

The smell hit me first.

That unmistakable mix of detergent, teenage sweat, and cologne he'd spray too heavily on days he wanted to impress someone. It was him. All of him, so sudden, so sharp, it brought me to my knees.

I pressed my face into your blue hoodie and breathed in as though oxygen depended on it.

And for a moment, I existed in the past, suspended in memory's fragile mercy.

The Drawer Full of Fragments

Later, I found myself opening drawers I had avoided. Slowly, reluctantly, as though each one contained a fragile creature that might break if touched.

Inside:

- A half-used stick of deodorant

- A crumpled movie ticket

- Headphones with one side broken

- A spare key he never remembered to return

- A note he wrote to himself: *"Don't forget to breathe."*

That last one stopped me.

Why would a nineteen-year-old need to remind himself to breathe?

Or had it been a joke? A scribble, a moment of teenage humor.

I'll never know.

It is one of grief's cruelties: so many questions become permanent echoes with no possible answers.

But I placed the note gently in my palm, whispering,

"I'm trying, baby. I'm trying too."

The Decision That Haunted Me

People mean well when they say,

"You don't have to keep everything."

They don't understand that *everything feels like something.*

Every sock, every photo, every worn-out shoe: a piece of a life that should still be unfolding.

How do I choose what parts of my child's life to preserve?

How do I decide which memories are worthy of staying, and which ones must be let go?

It feels cruel.

It feels impossible.

It feels like choosing which moments of him get to live.

In the end, I didn't decide in one day.

I made hundreds of small ones over months, each one carried like a stone in my hands.

And that's how grief often works:

not through grand gestures,

but through slow courage

In tiny acts.

The Box I Labeled "Keep"

There was one box, simple, brown, unremarkable, that became the heart of mourning.

Inside it, I placed:

- The blue hoodie that still smelled like you

- Your favorite photo of the two of us

- Your baby brush and rattle (we kept over the years)

- Your watch, still set to the time you last checked it

- A small toy car from your childhood, its paint chipped and beloved

As I placed each item inside, I whispered a quiet blessing, my hands trembling not from weakness, but from the weight of love.

I closed the box gently.

Not to bury you.

Not to forget you.

But to create a place where your memory could rest without crushing me.

The Moment I realized your Things Don't hold you, Your Love Does

Weeks later, I walked past your room again, and something felt different.

The air still ached, but it no longer suffocated.

Carl: A Mother's Love, A Life Remembered

The space still held you, but it no longer trapped me inside the loss.

And in the soft quiet of that moment, I understood something; grief had been trying to teach me all along:

You don't live in the fabric of that blue hoodie.

You don't live in a drawer, or a closet, or a box.

You live in me, your mother.

In the way, I still speak your name with tenderness.

In the way my love for you pulses through every breath, even the broken ones.

In the way your laughter echoes in your memory loud enough to warm the coldest days.

Your things may grow heavy.

Your love never will.

Because grief changes.

Loss shifts.

But a mother's love

that is forever.

Carl's baby brush and rattle

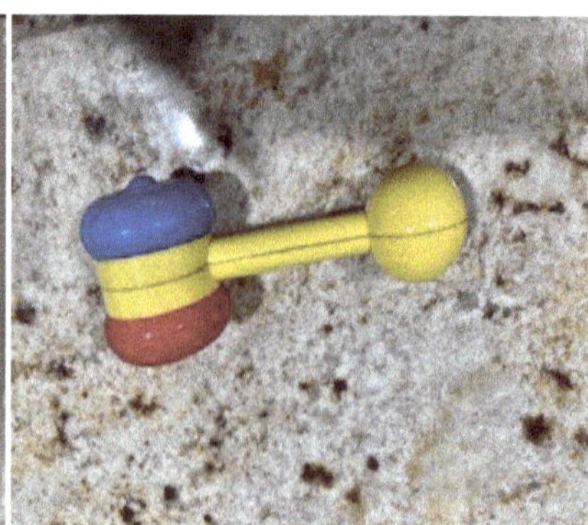

Chapter 13

Building a Legacy Out of Love

Turning grief into purpose through a mother's enduring love.

There are moments in grief when the world feels unbearably small.

The house feels smaller.

The days feel smaller.

My own body feels too small to hold the weight of what I've lost.

But then there are moments, rare, unexpected, when something inside me stirs, like a soft pulse reminding me that love, even broken love, still wants to move. Still wants to reach. Still wants to become something larger than pain.

The foundation began as one of those moments.

Just a flicker at first.

A whisper of an idea.

A sense that your life, your light, your kindness should not end in the moment that broke everything.

I named it the Carl David Richardson Foundation, Inc.

Just writing your name in the paperwork made my hands tremble.

Seeing it in print, official, permanent, felt like placing your heart back into the world.

It was the first time since losing you that I felt something like hope.

The Idea That Saved Me

I didn't start the foundation because I was strong.

I started it because I was breaking, and I needed a place for the pieces to go.

Grief is too heavy to hold alone.

Love is too powerful to stay trapped inside pain.

So, I began to imagine:

- scholarships for students like you

- support for families touched by violence and sudden loss

- community projects that carried your gentle spirit forward

- programs that would turn tragedy into transformation

- helping developmentally delayed children, your passion

These became my lifelines.

Not because they erased my grief, nothing ever could.

But because they gave my grief direction.

Purpose became a bandage for the wound.

Service became the breath I could count on when the nights were too long.

Helping others became the only way to feel like I was still mothering you.

Dr. Johann Richardson, PhD

Carl's Work With Children: Tutoring and Guidance

Carl, you spent time tutoring children in our neighborhood, offering patient, one-on-one support with homework, reading, problem solving, and school assignments. You believed every child deserved the chance to succeed, and you made time for them. You listened, you explained concepts with care, and you encouraged them until learning felt possible.

Your kindness reached beyond home and into classrooms. You volunteered at an elementary school in Queens, where you assisted an occupational therapist, helping children participate in activities and build confidence. Every conversation, every lesson, and every moment of encouragement became a small seed of growth planted in a child's future.

These experiences revealed the young man you were becoming. You moved through the world with compassion, responsibility, and a genuine desire to help others succeed.

After you went away, your spirit of compassion and purpose became the heartbeat of the Carl David Richardson Foundation, Inc. What began as your quiet dedication to helping others has grown into a mission that continues to touch lives every day.

Through the NYC Early Intervention Program, the Foundation provides children and families with emotional support and guidance, helping them access essential services such as physical, occupational, and speech therapy, as well as special instruction. The Women Helping Women Empowerment Group uplifts and strengthens women, offering mentorship, encouragement, and the belief that they can rebuild and thrive. The Men's Support Group cultivates brotherhood, healing, and accountability, creating a safe space for men to connect and grow together. The Conflict Resolution Program stands as a bridge toward peace, bringing people together through empathy, understanding, and respect.

Carl, your quiet strength lives on in every child who finds their voice, every woman who rediscovers her power, every man who learns to heal, and every community that chooses compassion over conflict. Your legacy continues to guide us, to lift others, to serve with love, and to remind us all of the power of giving back.

Healing in the Work

At first, I could barely say the words out loud:

"My son

his foundation

our mission"

Each phrase felt like it had to cross a field of broken glass before it reached my lips.

But over time, the work softened the sharp edges.

Every email I wrote,

every meeting I attended,

every plan sketched out on paper

they stitched me back together in small, almost invisible ways.

People would ask,

"How do you do it? How do you find the strength?"

I never told them the whole truth:

I don't have strength.

I have a mother's love.

And that is stronger than anything grief can take from me.

The more I worked, the more I felt you there.

Not as a memory fading, but as a presence guiding.

Some days I'd swear I heard you saying,

"I'm proud of you, Mom."

Carrying Your Name Forward

There was something sacred about seeing your name on the foundation's first letterhead.

Something only in watching travels into communities, into hearts, into lives you never got to meet.

Carl David Richardson.

A name that once belonged only to my child

now belonged to a mission

A mission born from your love, your laughter, your kindness, your dreams.

It gave your name wings.

And in doing so, I found my own.

Because a mother's grief can drown her

or it can become a river that flows outward, nourishing others.

  I chose the river.

How the Foundation Helped Me Cope

It didn't take the pain away.

It didn't fill the empty chair at the holidays.

It didn't silence the nights when the sorrow hit like a wave breaking over my chest.

But it did something else.

Something profound.

It reminded me that:

- Your life had meaning.

- Your story could help someone else survive.

- Your love didn't end when your life did.

- I could still mother you through the lives I touched.

The foundation gave my grief a purpose, a place to land, and a path to walk.

Instead of being swallowed by the loss,

I began to walk with it.

side by side

turning pain into fuel,

turning sorrow into service,

Turning your absence into presence.

I wasn't healed.

But I was held

by the mission,

by the community,

By the legacy of the boy who made me a mother.

And somewhere deep inside, I knew:

This is how you continue.

This is how I carry you.

This is how love becomes forever.

Dr. Johann Richardson, PhD

Carl David Richardson Foundation Early Intervention Program Office

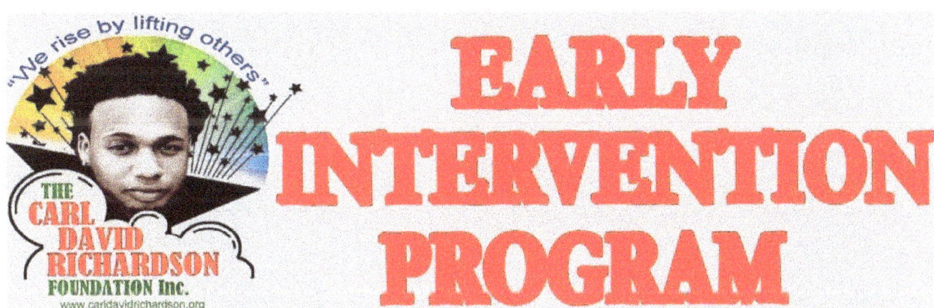

Carl: A Mother's Love, A Life Remembered

Highlights from events Presented by the Carl David Richardson Foundation, Inc.

Dr. Johann Richardson, PhD

Carl: A Mother's Love, A Life Remembered

Dr. Johann Richardson, PhD

Carl: A Mother's Love, A Life Remembered

64

Chapter 14

A Street Named for Carl David Richardson

Honoring a life of kindness and community by weaving a lasting legacy into the city's streetscape

My dear Carl, did you know there's a street in Queens that bears your name? Your mother advocated for you, my son; I wrote letters to let them know who you are and why the community needs to know about you. Right there on the corner of Merrick Boulevard and 228th Street in Laurelton, the city put up a sign that says Carl David Richardson Foundation Way.   Every time I pass it, I feel as though your spirit still walks these streets, smiling at the neighborhood you loved so much. It's the place where community still thrives, even in the bustle of the city, and now your name is part of that forever.

You were just nineteen, but you left behind a mark bigger than your years. Everyone remembers your kindness, how you'd rush to help without anyone asking, how you wanted to make things better for people. You worked hard, balancing school at St. John's Prep, college at Nassau, your job, and volunteering with the kids at PS 46. You never stopped giving.

After you were gone, I knew I had to do something to keep that light burning. That's why I started the Carl David Richardson Foundation, Inc. to teach young people that peace is strength, that conflicts can be resolved with understanding and respect. Through this work, your name keeps bringing people together, helping them find hope.

Councilman Donavan Richards spoke so beautifully at the ceremony. He said your story would inspire young people walking by, reminding them of what's possible, of the choice to live with compassion instead of anger. I knew then that he understood you the way I did.

Now, every time someone looks up at that sign, they'll see more than letters. They'll see love turned into action, sorrow turned into strength. You may have left this world too soon, my son, but your name, your heart, will live on in every corner of this community.

Carl's street naming ceremony

Chapter 15

The Quiet Rooms of Grief

Grief reshapes the inner landscape, creating quiet spaces for sorrow and love to coexist

Grief changes the architecture of my life.

There are rooms inside me now that didn't exist before

silent spaces shaped by pain, memory, and the echoes of moments I can never return to.

These rooms are not always dark.

Some are filled with soft light, warmed by memories that still know how to smile.

Others are shadowed, tender to the touch, as if the walls themselves remember the day my world broke.

This chapter of healing, if "healing" is even the right word, was not loud or dramatic.

It did not come with milestones or markers.

It arrived quietly, almost unnoticed, like sunlight slipping under a closed door.

It came in moments of stillness,

on mornings when I realized I hadn't woken up sobbing,

or afternoons when your name could float through my thoughts

without knocking the breath out of my chest.

These were the quiet rooms of grief

spaces within me where sorrow and love learned to sit beside each other.

A Room Called Acceptance, Though I Never Chose it

Acceptance is not surrender.

It is not an agreement.

It is not saying the loss is "okay."

Acceptance is simply the moment I stop fighting reality.

Because grief has already carved it into my bones.

This room was small at first.

Bare.

Fragile.

I entered it not by choice, but by exhaustion.

After months, years, of wrestling with the impossible truth,

My heart began to whisper:

You're gone from this world,

But you're not gone from me.

Standing in this room felt like standing on uneven ground.

Acceptance did not make the pain smaller.

It only made it less surprising.

It taught me how to carry the weight.

Without collapsing under it.

Dr. Johann Richardson, PhD

A Room Filled with Memories That Don't Hurt the Same Way

There is a strange shift that happens over time.

Memories that once felt like open wounds

Begin to take on a different texture

still tender, still sacred,

But no longer sources of unbearable pain.

I found myself laughing softly at stories of you:

The things you used to say,

The way you would pretend to be annoyed when I hugged you too long,

The way your smile took up your whole face.

I could remember you without falling apart.

It wasn't that the grief disappeared,

It simply stepped aside for a moment.

To let the love breathe.

This room became my refuge.

A place where you lived

In full color.

A Room Made of Anger, and How I Learned to Walk Through It

Anger was the room I feared the most.

It pulsed with heat

rage at the unfairness,

Rage at the violence that stole you,

Rage at the world for not stopping its spin.

I avoided this room for months,

Terrified of what would happen if I let myself feel the full force of it.

But I discovered something:

Anger is not the enemy.

It is a companion that walks beside grief.

Anger said,

"This mattered."

"This was sacred."

"This should never have happened."

And once I stopped running from it,

I found a strange sort of strength waiting inside that room.

A fire that fueled the foundation,

A fire that kept me fighting for others,

A fire that refused to let your story be forgotten.

Anger softened over time,

becoming not a blaze,

But a steady flame.

A Room Where Tears and Peace Coexist

There were days when I cried quietly,

not from overwhelming heartbreak,

but from a softer ache

an ache of missing,

an ache of longing,

An ache of remembering how deeply I love you.

These tears were different.

They didn't crush me.

They cleansed me.

They washed away the fear that moving forward.

Meant not moving away from you.

In this room, I finally understood:

Grief is not something I get over.

It is something I learn to live with

like a second heartbeat,

A silent beat that belongs to you.

A Final Room, The One Where I Begin Again

This room looked unfamiliar at first.

Not because grief had vanished

But because hope had quietly stepped inside.

Hope didn't burst through the door.

It didn't announce itself.

It simply stood in the corner, gentle and patient,

Waiting for me to notice.

I began to rebuild myself here.

slowly,

carefully,

With the pieces of my life rearranged into a new shape.

A shape that held love and loss at the same time.

A shape that honored you.

A shape that allowed me to keep breathing.

I didn't leave grief behind.

I carried it with me.

But I carried it differently.

Not as a weight dragging me under,

But as a reminder of how deeply I can love.

The quiet rooms of grief

Became the quiet rooms of my heart.

And inside them,

Dr. Johann Richardson, PhD

Your presence echoed softly,

guiding me forward,

One tender step at a time.

A glimpse into the day we said goodbye

Chapter 16

Learning to Live Again Without Letting Go

Grief rewrites identity, revealing resilience and a new way to live with love

There comes a point in grief when I realize I am not the same person I was before, not even close.

Loss rewrites me.

Not suddenly, but slowly, word by word, breath by breath.

Some days I wondered if I was disappearing into my sorrow, becoming only the mother of a murdered son, as though the world could no longer see the woman who existed before the tragedy.

I missed her.

I mourned her too.

But in this chapter, quietly, gently, I began to discover a new version of myself.

One shaped by grief, yes,

But also by resilience, love, and a strength I never asked for but somehow grew into.

The First Time I Caught Myself Moving Forward

It didn't happen with a dramatic decision.

It wasn't a vow or a revelation.

It happened on an ordinary morning.

I was washing dishes, hands submerged in warm water, the hum of the world soft around me.

And I realized, almost startled by it, that for a few minutes, my mind had not been in pain.

I was simply *living*.

Not joyfully or effortlessly,

But living nonetheless.

It felt strange, almost disloyal,

Like stepping into sunlight after months in the dark.

But I didn't step back.

Because somewhere inside me, a new truth whispered:

Moving forward is not moving away.

My love remains.

I remain.

The Gentle Return of Desire

Grief steals desire.

Not just for joy, but for life itself.

There was a long time when I didn't want anything:

not laughter,

not company,

not plans,

Not dreams.

But then, tiny sparks appeared.

So small I almost didn't recognize them.

A craving for fresh air.

A longing to hear music I once enjoyed.

A wish to gather with people who loved me.

A sudden interest in something beautiful,

A sunrise, a flower, a child's laugh.

At first, I brushed these moments aside,

Afraid they meant I was "moving on,"

Afraid they erased something sacred.

But slowly, I let them in.

Because maybe, just maybe,

These moments weren't signs of forgetting

They were signs of survival.

Allowing Life to Touch Me Again

There is a moment in grief when life asks a simple but profound question:

May I come back in?

It came to me unexpectedly.

Maybe through the kindness of someone who held my hand.

Maybe through the foundation meetings that filled my days with purpose.

Maybe through whispers of laughter that didn't feel like betrayal anymore.

I didn't open the door all at once.

I cracked it

Cautious, trembling, and uncertain.

And life entered gently,

Without rushing me.

I allowed myself:

- to smile without apologizing

- to rest without guilt

- to dream small dreams

- to imagine a future that did not erase my past

I began to understand that living again.

Does not mean loving less.

The Strength I Never Saw Growing

Sometimes people told me,

"You are so strong."

I wanted to say:

"No. This is not a strength. This is survival."

But over time, I began to see it differently.

Strength wasn't the absence of tears.

It was the willingness to feel them.

Strength wasn't pretending to be okay.

It was showing up even when I wasn't.

Strength wasn't moving past the grief,

It was carried with grace.

And refusing to let it turn my heart to stone.

I didn't choose strength.

I grew it, unknowingly,

The same way a tree grows roots

Quietly, deeply, beneath the surface.

Where I Begin to Rejoin the World

This was not just a grand return,

No triumphant moment, no dramatic turning point.

It was subtle.

I answered calls again.

I left the house more often.

I let people hug me without stiffening.

I allowed myself moments of softness,

moments of curiosity,

Moments of peace.

Not because the pain was gone,

It never will be.

But because my heart discovered something astonishing:

I can live and grieve at the same time.

I can miss you fiercely.

And still build a life with open hands.

I can carry your memory.

not as a weight

But as a guiding light.

And slowly, so slowly I barely noticed,

My life started expanding again,

Stretching around the grief instead of collapsing under it.

I began to live, not despite the loss,

but with it,

through it,

As a mother who loves her son in a world that sometimes breaks

But still holds room for healing.

Carl's Farewell Salute, Mom always by your side

Chapter 17

When the World Expects You to Be "Okay"

Grief has its own pace; strength lies in honoring your truth, not society's timeline.

There comes a time in grief, not marked on any calendar, not circled on any date, when the world quietly decides that I should be "better" by now.

People stop checking in as often.

Their voices soften less when they ask how you're doing.

The pauses after I mention your name grow shorter.

Some conversations shift to lighter topics,

As if they're afraid my sorrow is contagious.

And without meaning to,

The world begins to expect my heart to have healed.

At the same pace, their attention has faded.

But my grief has its own timeline.

It's own unrushed rhythm.

It's own truth.

This chapter was about learning how to live in a world.

That kept asking me to move on,

While I was still learning how to breathe.

The Pressure to Appear Strong

I noticed it first in small comments:

"You're doing so well."

"You're so strong."

"He wouldn't want you to be sad."

"You have to keep living."

They meant well,

They always meant well.

But each phrase felt like a stone placed gently in my pocket,

Pulling me deeper into the water of expectations.

They didn't see the nights when I curled on the floor,

Holding the ache in my chest like a living thing.

They didn't see how saying your name still made my voice tremble.

They didn't see how mornings felt like climbing out of a canyon.

I never meant to fall into.

Being seen as strong became another weight to carry,

Another mask to hold in place.

But inside, I whispered to myself:

Strength is not the absence of tears.

Strength is carrying my love for you.

Through a world that cannot possibly understand.

The Unseen Battles

There were days when I functioned so well.

That people probably assumed I was healed.

I cooked.

I worked.

I participated in meetings.

I answered emails for the foundation.

I held conversations in grocery store aisles.

Without breaking down.

But what they didn't know

Was the quiet battle happening inside:

- how hearing a teenage boy laugh could bring tears to my eyes

- how certain songs felt like blades

- how watching families together triggered a soft ache under my ribs

- how joy and grief lived intertwined in every breath

I became an expert at moving through the world.

While carrying a heart still tender, still raw, still learning how to beat again.

Giving myself Permission to Not Be Okay

This was the hardest permission to grant,

harder than forgiving,

harder than accepting,

Harder than letting life begin again.

I had to give myself permission.

To be human.

To have days when the grief returned with sharp edges.

To cancel plans without apology.

To cry in the car and let the tears fall with no shame.

To have moments when the weight of missing you

Felt heavier than my own bones.

I learned that grief is not linear.

It is a tide,

sometimes gentle,

sometimes violent,

But always moving.

And I learned

that being "not okay."

Is not a weakness.

It is love.

It is remembrance.

It is the price of carrying a piece of you inside me.

Every single day.

Protecting my Healing

I began to understand

that part of surviving grief

is protecting my own heart from the world's impatience.

I learned to step away from conversations.

That minimized my loss.

I gave myself space

From people who expected me to "get over it."

I allowed myself boundaries,

Soft ones, firm ones, necessary ones.

Healing required quiet.

It required gentleness.

It required honoring my own timeline.

Instead of the world.

Sometimes healing meant

Closing my door and breathing alone.

Sometimes it meant

Surrounding me with those who spoke your name with warmth.

Sometimes it meant

letting the foundation work be my shelter,

my purpose,

My way of staying connected to you

While lifting others out of darkness.

This was how I protected the sacredness of my grief,

not by hiding it,

But by honoring it.

The Moment I Realized I Don't Owe the World "Okay"

There was a moment, quiet, private, important.

When something shifted inside me.

I realized that "okay" was not a destination,

not a finish line,

Not a requirement.

I didn't owe the world.

A neat version of my heartbreak.

I didn't owe them a smile.

On days when the weight was unbearable.

I didn't owe them a story.

With a clean ending.

I only owed myself the truth:

I am grieving.

I am healing.

I am remembering.

I am learning to live with love and loss.

Woven together in the same breath.

And that truth, raw, unpolished, honest,

Became my freedom.

From that moment on,

I carried my grief not as something to hide,

But as something sacred.

A testament to the depth of my love for you, my son.

A reminder that my heart, shattered but still beating,

Was brave enough to continue.

I was not "okay."

Carl: A Mother's Love, A Life Remembered

I was something deeper.

Something real.

Something strong in a way the world could not define.

I was a mother

still loving her son

In a world that keeps moving forward,

and that love, steady and unbroken,

Will always be enough.

A mother's trip to Jamaica without her son

Chapter 18

The Quiet Work of Becoming Again

Grief transforms through small moments of willingness, becoming a quiet, evolving journey of becoming.

Grief changes over time, but it never disappears. It softens in some places and hardens in others. It becomes a landscape I learn to walk through with new muscles and a different kind of breath. By the time I reached the phase of my journey that would become this chapter, I could sense something shifting inside me, not a miracle, not a sudden burst of light, but something smaller, quieter. A willingness, a tiny inclination toward life again.

Some days, that willingness looked like opening the blinds instead of sitting in the dark. Other days, it was answering a phone call instead of letting it ring. And sometimes, it was the boldness of stepping outside without feeling like the world was made of broken glass.

But it was fragile. I was fragile.

The world still felt too loud, too careless, and too unkind. I often wondered how I could ever coexist with a society that kept spinning while my own planet had fallen out of orbit. Still, something inside me insisted on trying.

I began by allowing myself to participate in small joys, nothing extravagant. A warm cup of tea that I sipped slowly, letting the steam lift into my face like a blessing. A walk around the block where I could feel the sun warming the crown of my head. A conversation with someone who spoke softly and didn't rush me. These were my early attempts at re-entering the world, at learning how to carry my grief without collapsing under it.

One of the most profound shifts happened in the moments I spoke your name without breaking. I didn't whisper it anymore. I didn't choke on the syllables. I began to say it fully, firmly: Carl, my son, my heart, and my reason for everything that came next.

That's when I noticed something else stepping forward inside me, a resolve I didn't know was waiting.

I had survived the shock, the silence, the unbearable loneliness. I had survived the days when breathing felt like dragging my body through water. I had survived the nights when memories became knives.

What remained now was the question I had avoided for so long:

What do I do with this pain?

What do I do with this love?

I began to understand that grief needed motion, not to outrun it, but to keep it from swallowing me whole. It needed purpose, not to erase the loss, but to give the loss a place to live.

That realization became the quiet, powerful start of a new chapter of my life, one not defined by tragedy, but shaped by how I chose to respond to it.

I wasn't healed. I wasn't whole. But I was becoming.

And in becoming, I learned, it's its own kind of miracle.

 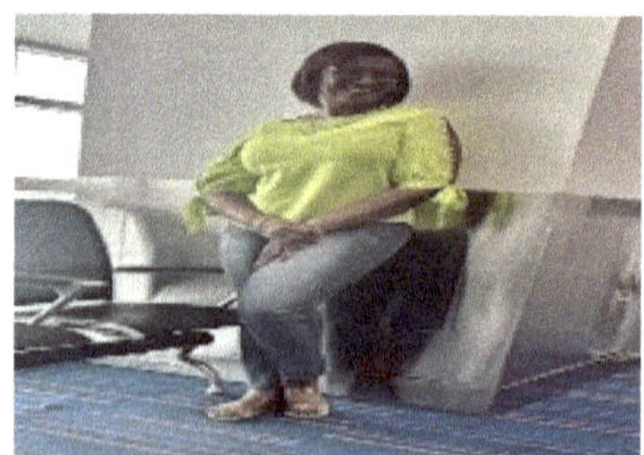

Chapter 19

When the World Begins to Notice MY Strength

Grief transforms identity, carving strength from love and survival.

There comes a moment in every grieving mother's journey when the world begins to reflect back to her something she cannot yet see in herself.

For me, that moment arrived gradually, like dawn creeping along the edge of the horizon, unsure whether it was welcome.

People began to tell me I was "strong."

At first, the word felt like an insult.

Strong?

How could anyone call me that when I still woke in the middle of the night, reaching out for a child who would never come home? How could I be strong when some days I barely stepped outside without trembling? When a mother's love, my love, still ached like an open wound?

But slowly, like a tide wearing down stone, I realized what they meant.

Strength wasn't about the absence of pain.

It was about surviving it.

It was about showing up, bleeding, trembling, tired, and still choosing to rise.

I didn't recognize it then, but the world did.

They saw the way I carried Carl's memory with dignity, refusing to let his name fade. They saw how I spoke of him with tenderness instead of bitterness, how I kept his light alive even when shadows threatened to swallow me.

But the truth was more complicated.

There were days I wanted to disappear.

Days when the grief sat on my chest like a weight I could not lift.

Days when I felt guilty for smiling, for enjoying a moment, for forgetting, if only for a breath, that my heart had been shattered.

And yet, even on those days, something in me kept moving.

I didn't realize it at the time, but the world watches the ways grieving mothers move. It watches the way we refuse to surrender, the way we turn pain into language, memory into motion, and brokenness into compassion.

That's when people started coming to me.

Some approached quietly, cautiously, as if they were hoping I would make the first move. Others came with tears already in their eyes. They told me about their own losses, parents, partners, siblings, and children. They asked me how I survived. They asked where I found the strength.

I never felt qualified to answer.

I was still learning myself.

But I understood something essential:

Grief recognizes grief.

It sees itself in another person's eyes, and sits down beside them without needing an explanation.

So I listened.

I held hands.

I prayed with strangers.

I let myself become a source of comfort, even when I felt small and fragile.

And strangely, helping others helped me.

Every story shared with me reminded me that love never dies, it transforms, it repurposes itself, and it becomes fuel for someone else's healing. And as people opened up to me, I began to see what I had become without realizing it:

I had become a witness.

A guide.

A living testimony of a mother who refused to crumble.

But most importantly, I had become someone who believed, despite everything, that my life still held meaning.

Not because the pain had faded, but because I had allowed it to shape me instead of destroy me.

By the time the world began to call me "strong," I finally understood that strength wasn't something I earned. It was something grief carved out of me.

And in the quiet spaces of my soul, I knew this:

Every ounce of strength I had was born from the love of my son.

Feeling Carl's presence in his room

Chapter 20

Carrying His Light Forward

Grief transforms pain into purpose, creating new meaning and a living legacy

There are moments when grief feels endless, stretching on like a road with no horizon.

And then there are moments when grief transforms, when it becomes something you can carry instead of something that holds you.

For me, that transformation came through the foundation.

The Carl David Richardson Foundation, Inc. became more than paperwork, meetings, or programs. It became a lifeline, a way to channel heartbreak into purpose, sorrow into service, and love into action.

Every child, every family helped, every program launched, it was as if a part of Carl continued to breathe in the world.

Through the foundation, his light, his kindness, his laughter, his boundless compassion kept moving, even though his presence in my arms was gone.

Finding Purpose Amid Pain

When I first began the work, I was fragile.

Every letterhead, every application, every phone call felt like I was risking too much of my heart. But slowly, something remarkable happened: the work started to heal me.

Helping others gave me a reason to get out of bed in the morning.

It gave my grief a structure, a rhythm, a place to go.

Instead of letting sorrow consume me, I poured it into something tangible, something that could grow, that could touch lives that could honor Carl in the truest sense.

I realized that a mother's love doesn't end when a child dies.

It changes shape.

It becomes advocacy.

It becomes protection.

It becomes hope for others who might be walking the same shadowed path I once did.

Moments That Still Take My Breath

Sometimes, even as the foundation flourished, grief would sneak in unexpectedly.

A parent would call me, tears in their voice, telling me how helping their child receive services had changed their child's life.

A person would tell me a story about someone inspired by Carl's kindness.

A young person would call, sharing stories on how the foundation has given thcm hope.

In those moments, I could feel Carl's presence, sharp, immediate, comforting.

I could almost hear his voice whispering,

"Mommy, you're doing it. You're keeping us alive."

And I would cry, not out of despair, but out of the fullness of love.

Out of the beauty of knowing that you were still here, still making a difference, still guiding me.

Learning to Live with Purpose

The foundation became my anchor.

Through it, I discovered that living again didn't mean leaving Carl behind.

It meant carrying him forward.

I learned that grief doesn't have to be a prison.

It can be a compass.

A map for how to continue loving when life has shifted its course.

Every meeting I attended, every child I helped, every family I comforted, I was teaching myself something vital:

I could grieve and create at the same time.

I could ache and hope simultaneously.

I could honor you and live for you.

A Mother's Mission

Carl's life, though tragically short, left a mark too significant for death to erase.

Through the foundation, I found a way to ensure that your story, your purpose, and your light continue.

Every act of service became a thread in a tapestry that could not be undone.

Every tear shed became proof that love endures.

The pain of losing you never disappears, but it evolves.

It shapes me,

guides me,

Teaches me that living is not about forgetting, but about carrying, nurturing, and transforming love into life.

And so, each day, I rise with intention.

Each day, I continue the work that honors you.

Each day, I whisper your name, and it feels like a prayer, a promise, and a mission all at once.

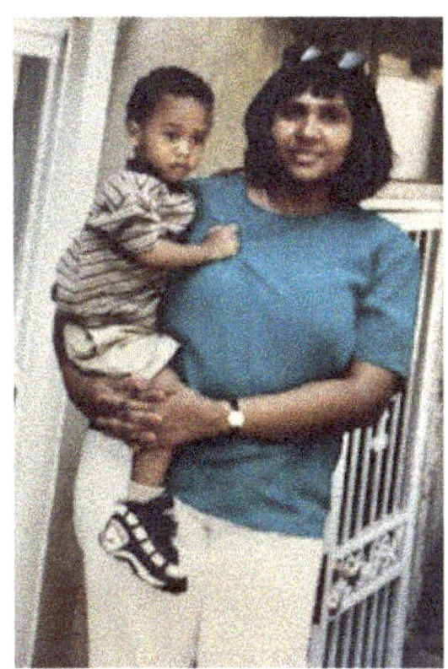 

Chapter 21

The Threads That Bind Us

Grief weaves a tapestry of love and loss that shapes and sustains the heart.

Grief is not a single moment.

It is a tapestry.

Each thread is a memory, a feeling, a sound, a smell, a glance, a laugh.

Some threads are bright, vibrant, sparkling with joy.

Some threads are dark, raw, and heavy with loss.

But together, they form the story of a life lived, a love shared, a connection that death cannot sever.

I have learned that these threads are not just woven into my memories; they are woven into me.

They shape the way I breathe, the way I speak, the way I hold the world in my arms.

And they bind me to you in ways the world will never see, but I feel in every heartbeat.

The Strength of a Mother's Heart

There is a quiet power in being a mother to a child who has died.

It is a power born of love, so deep it cannot be measured.

It is a courage that surfaces in the stillest, most unexpected moments:

- When I wake in the night and whisper my child's name.

- When I hold back tears in public, not because I do not want them to flow, but because I am practicing patience with myself.

- When I speak to strangers about their own grief and offer solace, even while my own heart feels cracked and empty.

Being a mother after loss means living in a paradox:

I am broken, yet whole.

I ache, yet I create.

I grieve, yet I hope.

Finding Meaning in the Darkness

The foundation, the people I meet, the lives we touch, and these are not replacements for what I have lost.

They are something else entirely:

A way to make the loss matter.

A way to ensure that your life, your laughter, your light, continues to ripple through the world.

A way to transform despair into purpose, love into action, sorrow into something that can guide others.

Through this work, I have discovered that meaning is not found in erasing pain.

It is found in standing with it, walking beside it, and using it to shape the world in ways that honor the life that was lost.

Moments Where I Feel Him Still

Some days, the threads feel so strong I swear you are near:

- In the laughter of a child who reminds me of you.

- In a soft breeze that brushes my cheek, warm and familiar.

- In the words of a parent whose life has been touched by the foundation, who calls your name with gratitude and reverence.

I feel you in these moments, not as a shadow of what I have lost,

But as a presence, a guide, a reminder that love does not end in death.

The Promise I Carry

Carl, my son, my heart, my life,

I carry your story in everything I do.

I carry it in the foundation, in the laughter we inspire, in the hope we offer.

I carry it in my quiet moments, when I whisper your name and feel your spirit close.

This is my promise:

To live fully, even while carrying grief.

To honor you, not with words alone, but with action.

To keep your light alive in a world that sometimes forgets how precious it is to hold a life, a child, a heart.

I have learned that grief and love can coexist.

That sorrow can fuel purpose.

That loss can shape a life not diminished, but made profoundly meaningful.

And in carrying you forward, Carl, I have found a way to breathe again.

Not despite your absence,

But because of your love, your life, and your light continue to guide me every day.

Carl with dad and mom

When Kevin, Your best friend, stayed by our side and became family

Chapter 22

Love That Never Ends

A mother's love transforms loss into an enduring legacy of light and purpose.

I have learned that a mother's love does not end with death.

It does not fade.

It does not shrink.

It transforms.

It becomes something both tangible and invisible, something that shapes every breath I take, every step I make, and every choice I live with.

Carl, my son, you are everywhere in my life now.

In the quiet mornings when the sun touches my face.

In the sound of laughter that reminds me of yours.

In the gentle sway of a tree, in the shimmer of a raindrop.

You are not gone, you are here, woven into the fabric of my existence.

The Legacy of a Life Loved

Through the Carl David Richardson Foundation, Inc., your life continues to touch others in ways I could never have imagined.

Every family helped, every child inspired, every moment of kindness sparked by your story reminds me that even though the world feels cruel and unfair, love is stronger than absence.

You have taught me, Carl, that life is not measured by the number of breaths we take, but by the love we give, the joy we create, and the lives we touch.

Even in your absence, your purpose continues.

Living With an Open Heart

There are days when the ache hits fresh, sudden, and unbearable.

I do not pretend otherwise.

I do not hide my grief.

It is part of me, part of this journey, and it always will be.

But I have learned to carry it alongside hope, alongside love, alongside action.

I have learned that it is possible to grieve deeply and still engage fully with life.

To honor the past without being trapped by it.

To carry your memory with reverence, while still making room for moments of joy, connection, and even laughter.

Grief is not the absence of life; it is the measure of love.

The Quiet Strength of Continuance

I walk each day carrying both sorrow and gratitude.

I carry the knowledge that I have loved as fiercely as any mother could.

That I have nurtured, celebrated, and cherished a son whose time on this earth was far too short.

That I have transformed heartbreak into purpose.

That I have allowed your light to guide not only me, but countless others.

There will never be a day when I do not think of you.

There will never be a day when your name is not whispered in my heart.

But there will be days when I smile because of you.

Days when I take a small step forward because of you.

Days when I act with courage because your life, though brief, was brave, radiant, and full of meaning.

The Light You Left Behind

Carl, my beloved son, you live within every kindness I give, every step I take toward light. I will tell your story not just in words, but through the lives touched by our work, the hearts lifted through compassion, and the courage I find each day to keep moving forward.
I will remember you in laughter that heals and in quiet moments when grief softens into grace. Your presence guides me, in the choices I make, the people I love, and the hope I nurture in your name.
Though your time here was far too short, your impact endures, shaping me, teaching me, reminding me that even in loss, love expands. You are my son, my heartbeat, the soul behind my purpose. And I promise: your love will echo, always.

And so, my sweet Carl, I'll keep following your light, knowing it leads me forward, even as part of my heart lingers where you are.

What Love Refuses to Let Die

I did not choose this journey.

I would have chosen laughter over tears, milestones over memorials, and a future filled with ordinary moments instead of anniversaries of loss. I would have chosen to watch my son grow into the man I knew he would become. But grief does not ask permission, and violence does not knock before it enters your life.

On March 27, 2014, my world split into a before and an after. Before, I was Carl's mother, proud, hopeful, and dreaming alongside my 19-year-old son. After, I became the mother of a murdered child, forced to learn a new language of sorrow that no one ever wants to speak.

For a long time, breathing felt like work. Living felt unfair. And hope felt like betrayal, betrayal of the love I had for Carl, betrayal of the depth of my pain. But grief has a way of teaching you truths you never wanted to learn. One of those truths is this: love does not die when a life is taken.

Love transforms. Carl David Richardson was not defined by how he died. He was defined by how he lived, by his laughter, his kindness, his dreams, and the space he occupied in the hearts of those who knew him. He was defined by the way his life continues to ripple outward, touching people he never met, changing outcomes he will never see, and inspiring work that now carries his name.

The Carl David Richardson Foundation, Inc. was not born out of strategy or ambition. It was born out of survival. It was born because I needed somewhere to put my pain so it would not destroy me. It was born because I realized that if my son's life was taken by violence, then his legacy would be claimed by purpose.

This foundation is my refusal.

My refusal to allow violence to have the final word.

My refusal to let grief become my grave.

My refusal to let Carl's name be spoken only in whispers and tears.

Instead, his name is spoken in classrooms where conflict is resolved instead of escalated. It is spoken in rooms where women are reminded of their strength. It is spoken in communities where healing is not just a dream, but a practice. Every program, every event, every life touched is a declaration: Carl mattered. And he still does.

Carl David Richardson. Always remembered. Always loved. Always with me.

Carl having dinner with his brother, his nice and dad

Dr. Johann Richardson, PhD

A MOTHER'S LOVE

A mother's love is a quiet, unyielding force, woven from endless devotion, sacrifice, and the depths of pain. It lives in the whispered echoes of her son's laughter, now silenced forever at 19, and in the heavy stillness of a home marked by his absence. This love is a sacred tether, holding on fiercely despite the unbearable weight of loss. No darkness, not even the cruelty of murder, can sever the bond forged by a mother's heart. It endures beyond explanation, resilient and unbreakable, an eternal flame that no sorrow can extinguish.

In the tender moments she reaches for him in dreams, the warmth of his touch lingers like the fading fragrance of a familiar hug. Her grief, raw and consuming, is the language of love itself, where every tear is both a wound and a testament to the depth of what she holds inside. A mother's love transforms pain into strength, sorrow into remembrance, and loss into an everlasting embrace that defies time and tragedy.

About the Author

Dr. Johann Richardson's love for her son, Carl, is a tender, unyielding force born from profound loss. When Carl, her 19-year-old son, was tragically taken from her by a senseless act of violence, an adult's failure to handle conflict, Johann's grief could have shattered her. But instead, it ignited a fierce determination: Carl's name would not fade into silence or sorrow. In the quiet moments, she remembers his laughter and kindness, how he gave selflessly, shoveling snow for elderly neighbors and donating blood to help others. Her heart aches with the absence of his touch, yet it is this very loss that sweeps her into action.

With deep love as her guide, Johann founded the Carl David Richardson Foundation, Inc., a living tribute to her son's spirit and dreams. The foundation channels her pain into purpose: the Women Helping Women Empowerment Group offers support and healing to women facing difficult struggles, while the Conflict Resolution Program aims to plant seeds of peace early in every school, believing that if children learn to resolve conflict with empathy and respect, tragedies like Carl's death can be prevented. The foundation also includes the NYC Early Intervention Program, which serves developmentally delayed babies from birth to 3 years of age, and a Men's Support Group that helps fathers like Johann's husband, Carl Sr., cope with grief and other challenges men face. Johann carries Carl within her always, whispering his name into the world, turning a mother's grief into a mission for hope and change. Her love is a light fierce enough to transform heartbreak into healing for countless others.

A Mother's Tribute

Carl was the light of our life, a son whose kindness and laughter filled every room he entered. Losing him so young, to a senseless act of violence, broke our hearts in ways words cannot express. Yet in that sorrow, our love for him grew even stronger, a fierce, enduring bond that drives us to keep his memory alive. Through the Carl David Richardson Foundation, we honor Carl's spirit by working to build a safer world where no other mother, father or family must face such pain. Carl's life was a gift, and his love remains our guiding light forever.

Dr. Johann Richardson, PhD

CARL DAVID RICHARDSON

Carl, you were an extraordinary and inspiring young man, intelligent, loyal, and deeply motivating. Your life touched and impacted countless people, leaving a profound legacy that will forever live on. We carry your memory in our hearts as we continue to celebrate the remarkable moments and enduring influence you have gifted us all.

With Gratitude

To everyone who has held Carl in their hearts
through prayers, presence, love, and quiet acts of kindness
thank you.

Thank you to our family, friends, and community, and to all who stood beside us during the most difficult moments of our lives. Your compassion carried us when words were not enough, and your support reminded us that we were not alone.

This book was created not only to remember Carl's life, but to honor the love he gave, the light he carried, and the legacy that continues through each person he touched. Though his time here was far too short, Carl's spirit lives on, in kindness, in courage, and in the commitment to lift others.

May his memory continue to inspire peace, purpose, and compassion in the lives of all who read these pages.

With love and enduring gratitude,

Dr. Johann Richardson
Carl's mother